THE HIJAB OF ZAINAB

Written & Illustrated by
Fatima Mahdi

First Published in 2024 by
Ahlulbayt Islamic Mission (AIM)

ISBN: 978-1-7384949-1-0

© AIM Foundation 2024

All rights reserved. No part of this publication may be reproduced, stored in a retrieval system, or transmitted in any form or by any means, digital, electronic, mechanical, photocopying, recording, or otherwise, or conveyed via the internet or a website without prior written permission of the publisher, except in the case of brief quotations embodied in critical articles and reviews.

 *Dedicated to the Lady of Light*
Sayyida Fatima Al-Zahra
Peace be upon her

I got out of bed and quickly ran down the stairs.
Mama and baba were in the living room
organising the decorations and chairs.

I shouted: "Mamma! I am so excited, the day has finally come.
I get to be just as special and as great as you, mum".

My mum replied: "Yes, my beautiful, that is right.
You are now a soldier in an important fight.
A leading star that will shine so bright.

You see Zainab, today is your big day,
you are turning NINE!
For other girls, this is ordinary.
But for us, Muslims it is holy and divine".

At this very age, Allah SWT called and said:
"My dear Zainab, you have a very important job ahead.
You are the one chosen to ensure my message is spread.
Just like the Prophets, you will pave the path for others to tread".

"Zainab" dad turned, smiled and looked me in the eye.
"If you think the hijab is special, can you tell me why?
Why do you want to wear the hijab on your head?
Do you not want to be like all the other girls instead?"

"Because Allah
LOVES ME"

      I quickly replied.
And He wants me to be free
and stay by his side".

"Baba, Allah made me and knows me best.
It's more than special, I am very very blessed".

"Plus baba, you know the answer better than me.
You've showed me the beauty of the hijab
even before the age of three".

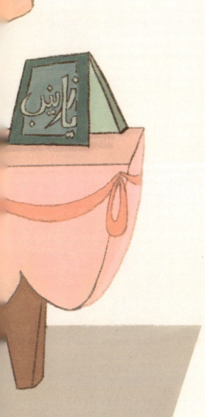

Mum then jumped in and she asked:
"Are you sure you are ready for this great task?
Are you not worried about what others may think or
the difficult questions they may ask?"

"Others! Worried?!"

I thought out loud.
"It is only God that I want to make proud".

"You raised me to never follow and always LEAD.
What others think I pay no heed".
Mum and dad nodded and agreed.

"Yes Zainab, Allah that loves and cares for us
knows what is best.
Why would we ever worry about the rest".

"You both have taught me right and I have a lot to say.
But the Adhan is near and we must prepare to pray".

As I was about to leave, my older brother walks in.
He looks around and says: "I have a few questions.
Where do I begin?"

"First of all, should you not wait a little bit longer?
Until you're older and your faith is stronger?"

Youssef, I laughed. "I know you're making fun. Do you know more than the creator of the heavens, Earth and sun?"

"Was it not just the other day that you were telling me the importance of following Allah's way?

Or else we will fail and go astray?

We are not smarter than our creator. His knowledge will always be much much greater".

Zainab,
you are definitely worthy.
You have swiftly passed the test.
"We were trying to challenge you", they all confessed.
Now, we must go prepare and get dressed.

Excited! I ran into my room and I closed the door.
My prayer mat already laying there on the floor.
I made my wudu and put on my prayer clothes.
The happiness I was feeling, only Allah knows.

I looked in the mirror and to myself I said:
"The banner of Islam now lays on my head.
Thank you Allah for this new path ahead".

I then admired my hijab and whispered aloud:
"Sayyida Zainab, I promise to make you proud".

The guests started to arrive; one after the other.
My family, friends, neighbours and my beautiful grandmother.
She has also been the perfect example for me.
She has showed me how a true Muslim should be.

In her I see Allah's kindness and love.
She reflects beauty from above.
As soon as she saw me, she hugged me so tight.
"My Zainab, are you ready for your speech tonight?"
"Yes teta, you have helped me so much. I think I'll be just right".

The next few hours we played, we spoke, we ate.
My mum's food was so delicious!
There was nothing left on anyone's plate.
It was then I realised that it was getting late.

I asked my dad to gather everyone around.
And suddenly there was not a single sound.

I began with Bismillah as we always do.
Followed by not one salawat, but rather two.

Speaking in front of a crowd has never been a favourite of mine.
But now with my hijab, I felt calm, I felt fine.

Thank you all for coming to my Takleef. I will try to keep my speech very brief.

"You see, when **Allah** created us and put us on this Planet called Earth.

He **PROTECTED** and **CARED** for us well before our birth.

He is the one who cures us when we are ill.
We SEE, WALK and TALK
through His will.

Allah knows us more than our mum and dad.
He is with us when we are
HAPPY, AFRAID, WORRIED OR SAD.
And of course he knows what is good for us and what is bad.
So, whatever Allah tells us to do
we must be confident and follow through."

"You see, the hijab is not just a cloth that I wear.
It is not just a covering for my hair.
It is the reason we still have
FASTING, HAJJ,
QURAN AND PRAYER."

On the day of Karbala, the enemy thought they had won.
Yazid thought Islam was over and the battle was done.
But, it was Sayyida Zainab who ensured that the fight
for our religion had only just begun.

When Sayyida Zainab lifted Imam Hussain's body to the sky.
It was the flag of Islam that she was raising high.
And this flag has now been

Gifted to you and I.

"I am honored and proud to wear the flag of Islam on my head.
Like Sayyida Zainab, my role is to ensure the truth is spread.
And follow what Allah has commanded and said.

How fortunate am I, how fortunate are you.
That we publicly raise the flag of Hussain
which is the flag of Islam too.

Our hijab is the flag, so let it be known.
We are the media and Islam's backbone.

With my hijab I am now stronger, smarter and wiser.

I am powerful! I am free!

I am the perfect example for all to see!

Allah chose me to be the flag bearer, the voice.
I am Allah's representative.

I am His choice."

"Society expects us to follow what we are told.
Boys, fashion, influencers or whatever is being sold.
But I think for myself! I cannot be controlled.
I have divine principles to uphold.

Like the cape of a hero, I will wear my hijab, proud.
I AM A MUSLIM, CLEAR AND LOUD.
I have been given the most important role.
To wake up society and free my soul.
My hijab is the enemy's greatest threat.
I am a constant reminder that they cannot forget.

As the martyrs have said, my hijab is more
important than the blood that they shed.
It is through my hijab that Allah's path will be lead.
It is through my hijab that the truth will be spread.
It is through my hijab that noble generations will tread.
So, I will wear my flag proud on my head!"

Thank you all again for coming today.
This is a glimpse of why I choose

Allah's Way

Milton Keynes UK
Ingram Content Group UK Ltd.
UKRC030917230624
444480UK00005B/27